Love
War
Life

Poems by
Tom Morton

Silver

Pullet Press

Love War Life © 2021 Tom Morton

Silver

Pullet Press
Clovis, CA

Production Assistance provided by HBE Publishing

All rights reserved. No part of this book may be used or reproduced in any manner whatsoever without written permission from the publisher, except in the case of brief quotations embodied in critical articles or reviews.

ISBN 978-1-952467-08-0 Trade Paperback
ISBN 978-1-952467-09-7 Ebook

November 2021

Acknowledgments

Writing is a lonely endeavor, but all writers have a support system. Mine consists of many friends and family. Among them are my mentor, Janice Stevens; my surrogate sisters and fellow authors: Anne Biggs, Karen Moore, Kathy Gorman, and Gayle Taylor-Davis.

Peggy and Dan Dunklee, and the staff at Clovis Book Barn, whose expertise and cooperation was invaluable.

The good folks at The Clovis Old Town Café for their never empty coffee cup.

Thank you all for making LOVE WAR LIFE possible.

Contents

LOVE

ALWAYS	3
SO IT IS	4
AGAIN	5
ROSES	6
SIDE BY SIDE	8
THANK YOU	10
CAN'T CAN	11
YOU AND ME	12
REMEMBER	13
WILD THING	14
YOU	15
HAWAII	16

WAR

PTSD 21

GENERATION WARS 22

TOUR 24

MASTER OF DETACHMENT 26

LIFE

A LOVE STORY	33
JACK	34
CONFIRMED	35
ALL LOVES	36
SECOND GUESSES	37
MY FRIEND JACK	38
A CHARM	40
ENJOYMENT	42
ONCE AGAIN	43
WHAT THE…	44
SUNRISE SUNSET	45
THE SEARCH	46
ON THE STREETS	47
AGE	48
CHOICES	49
About the Author	51

LOVE

ALWAYS

Yes

The best

Is yet

To come

You

By my side

Better not worse

Sweet not bitter

Fine wine to sip

Grace together

Not old

Anymore

In love

Always

SO IT IS

Sweet nectar

Attracts bees

So it is

For me

With you

So it is

With our love

Sweetness of your nectar

Lures me

So it is for us

Our love

AGAIN

Great sorrow

Never to

See you

Again

Great happiness

To see you

Again

Nothing to offer

Again

Only me

And

All my love

Again

ROSES

My roses glow

All the many colors

One shines the brightest

Lavender

Bursts with the enchantment

Of love at first sight

Orange

Burns with desire and enthusiasm

Passionate excitement

Becomes

Ardent romance

White

Shines the innocence

Of a new beginning

A marriage

Of honor

And

Reverence

One of remembrance

Yellow

Glows full of true friendship

One held

Near

And

Dear

Pink

Blooms of grace

Elegance

Admiration

Joy

Red

Bursts with love

Dearest of all

Beautiful perfection

The strongest of all

These are the many things

You mean to me

These are what

You are

To me

For me

My rose

SIDE BY SIDE

Loved you then

Love you now

Never stopped

As promised

Teens when first we loved

Side by Side

Always

I wonder

In the back of my mind

Would life have been different

Better or worse

Side by side

Lived and loved

Worked and played

Fought a war

All so hard

Would have been easier

Side by side

Success and failure

Would life have been sweet or bitter

Side by side

Always loved

As once professed

As good then

As good now

With you by my side

You ever wonder

How life might have been

Better

The same

At least

Not worse

Do you think

With you by my side

From where we were

To where we are

Have you ever been

Where I've been

Done anything I've done

Ever wonder

What would have been

With us

Side by Side

THANK YOU

I smile constantly

I laugh more than enough

Happiness fills my life

Each day holds

So much promise

Because

Of

You

CAN'T CAN

You hurt

I can't make it go away

I can't take it away

I can't make you feel better

I can't help you heal

Love you

I can

YOU AND ME

I drift off thinking of you

I sleep dreaming of you

I awake wanting you

You excite me

You bring out

The best in me

I know you love me

I love you

I adore you

I worship you

You are everything

To me

REMEMBER

Once

Us

Together

Passion

Love

Hope

Split

Apart

Alone

Lost

Loveless

Hopeless

Love

Elusive

WILD THING

Your wild side

You say not you

Is you

Been there

Once before

Loved it

Scared you

Not norm

Still think not

Liked it

Wanted it

Since then

Safer

Do what is expected

Dream of the unexpected

YOU

I feel sad

You excite

I feel old

You turn back time

Fire of passion gone

You rekindle it

Faith wanes

You restore it

I love

You

HAWAII

Day dreaming on Waikiki Beach

Thought of the day

She walked into his room

Dressed in a sexy smile

She drew closer at a sultry pace

Firm youthful breasts

Swayed side to side

Her love thirsty eyes

Fixed on his

Burned with desire

Loving expectations

Sheer joy

The same in his eyes

Message clear

Understood

Welcomed

Loved

Pace became more

Confident

Determined

Loving

Moved toward him

Onto his lap she climbed

You like?

Pulled her face to his

Whispered

I love you!

Kissed her

ALOHA!

WAR

PTSD

Suppress

Bury deep

Ignore

Erupts

Still alive

Buried deep

Part of me

Bubbles up

Who I am

No vows

But

Till death

Do us

Part

GENERATION WARS

Revolutionary

Freedom

Civil

Freedom for all

World War I

End all

World War II

Greatest generation

Glorious

Korea

Ignored generation

Forgotten

Cold War

Nukes

Posturing

Fear

Viet Nam

Stop communism

Strike a blow for democracy

Be a hero

Go to Viet Nam

No problem

Consider it done

Neat

Clean

Quick

Over soon

Surprise

58,000

Plus

TOUR

      Home

        U.S.

          May not drink

          Cannot vote

Away

        Viet Nam

          May kill

          Could die

      Jungle

       Hot

       Humid

Monsoon

        Wet

       Soaked

      Guns fire

      Bullets zip

     Artillery blasts

      Shells burst

    Explosions deafen

     Bones break

     Blood spurts

     Bodies shred

Flesh burns

Acrid air

Scarred

Lands

Bodies

Faces

Shattered lives

Crushed souls

No one dies

All killed

Mothers wail

Children cry

All mourn

Sadness seethes

Girlfriends cry

Wives weep

Mothers sob

All grieve

Death
Ashes
Stench

Home

No

One

Cares

MASTER OF DETACHMENT

Young

Viet Cong

Dead

We did it

Shot him up

Happy

Hear his mother

Wail

Her anguished face

Regret

Emotions   *NOT GOOD DETACH*

Truck

Full of Marines

Dead

Mourn

Emotions   *NOT GOOD DETACH*

Wounded

Worry

C.O.

Killed

Grieve

Emotions   *NOT GOOD DETACH*

Bru village

Mortared

Anger

Mother

Legs blown off

Compassion

Three children

Faces

Tears sear

Heartbreak

Mother's eyes

Blank

Children scream

Sympathy

Emotions   *NOT GOOD IN COMBAT*

Now

Detachment

A habit

I

Must

Break

LIFE

A LOVE STORY

Loved her

Wanted her

Couldn't have her

Hello Smith and Wesson

JACK

She thought

She knew him

He thought

He knew her

They did not

Know Jack

Jack knows best

Good luck

CONFIRMED

From the gut

Through the heart

Come the words

From the love

Back

Come the words

To your heart

Then you know

In your gut

Truth

ALL LOVES

Drifts off

Thinks of her

Sleeps

Dreams of her

Awakes

Wants her

Excites him

Loves her

Worships her

Adores her

There's

The door

Next

SECOND GUESSES

Sometimes

In the middle of the night

Sometimes

In the morning

Often

During the day

Doubt creeps in

Questions pop up

Some answers

Easy

Some answers

Hard

Smooth times

Unscathed

Rough times

Banged up

Beaten and bruised

All worth it

Keep going

Not over

Yet

MY FRIEND JACK

My friend Jack

And I go way back

We worked together

Laughed together

Even played together

And suffered together

At the same salt mine

Jack made an early escape

Lucky knave

He had fun

I continued to slave

He went away

I stayed

Years went by

Then his wife died

He needed some laughter in his life

Turned out he played cribbage

As did I

We knew no one else

Who played

Now and then

We got together

Laughed

Played

And counted

Fifteen - two

Fifteen - four

And a double double's a dozen

Pegged each other to death

So it seemed

No matter the count

No matter the score

No matter who won

The score was always

Twenty-nine

A perfect hand

With the right Jack

My friend Jack

A CHARM

Touched my soul

Took it back

All that remained

A black hole

Of despair

Touched by another

Damaged by bad memories

Loved twice

Hurt twice

Cared too much

Love

Elusive

Not elusive

Can be elusive

Do I avoid it

For the bad memories

Depression and despair

Cared too much

The black hole

Consumed once again

Touched a third time

Sunshine in the darkest places

During the darkest hours

Of depression

Once elusive

Now envelopes

Love the third

ENJOYMENT

My cigars

I enjoy

I enjoy

My booze

My wife

I love

I love

My life

I could do no better

Better than this

It doesn't get

ONCE AGAIN

The sun rose

Again

Dew formed

As before

Tree sprouted

Anxious to grow

A flower

Bloomed

Once again

As once before

Yet

Once again

WHAT THE…

Never enough time

Runs out

Starts again

What the…

Runs out

Too quick

What the…

Live

Work

Plan

Live more

Work harder

Plan again

Retire

Time enough

Runs out

Again

What the…

Dead

SUNRISE SUNSET

Sunrise

I am blessed

To wake up

Each day

To

Work and play hard

Laugh and love

I am blessed

Sunset

THE SEARCH

His lips pressed on hers

She felt his love

His warmth

His tongue parted her lips

Heat surged through her body

Her femininity about to burst in flames

Searched for his masculinity

To quench the fire

ON THE STREETS

Stupid drivers

I hate

Why I hate

Stupid drivers

Stupid drivers are

Dangerous drivers

Dangerous drivers

Cause crashes

Crashes

Maim and kill

Bring

pain and sorrow

Not smartest driver

Am I

A stupid driver

I hope not

AGE

Who said the best is yet to come

Where are the golden years

What happened to youth

Where did all the time go

When did I get old

When did the laugh lines become wrinkles

How does the fine wine fit in

Can the graceful part please start

I don't want to be an old fart

I don't want to be an old anything

CHOICES

That or which

Choosing is a bitch

Who or whom

For error there is no room

To or too

Wait

There is a third

Two

So to, too or two

To choose is tough

Too

Or is it to

Or maybe two

Two to choose

Is two to many

Or two too many

To — Two — Too

Who — Whom

That — Which — Witch

To choose

Still a bitch

Better to be a math major

About the Author

Tom Morton was born in Oakland, California. His dad's naval career allowed him to experience life on various naval bases — Washington, D.C., Guam, and Japan.

San Diego was home from junior high through college. When he wasn't playing other sports, he spent his time at the beaches of Southern California or Baja, ride, ride, riding the wild surf.

Tom has had many careers: short order cook, pizza slinger, Italian restaurant chef, newspaper distributor, TV news anchor, TV director, producer and writer, real estate agent and video production. He retired from a large government agency as a program/management analyst.

Tom met his wife, Fran, while working at a Fresno TV station. They married a few years later. Animal lovers, they have fostered many dogs and cats since then.

Tom and Fran have two children and two grandchildren.

He is also the author of WISKEY TANGO FOXTROT, REMEMBRANCES OF MY SERVICE IN THE MARINES